EMPIRES

Books by RICHARD MOORE

A Question of Survival
Word from the Hills: A Sonnet
  Sequence in Four Movements
Empires

Ontario Review Press Poetry Series

EMPIRES

Poems by
Richard Moore

Preface by
X.J. Kennedy

Ontario Review Press
Princeton, New Jersey

"Burr" and "Gould" first appeared in
The Georgia Review, "Archimedes" in *The Southern Review.*

Copyright © 1969, 1973, 1974, 1981 by Richard Moore
Preface © 1981 by X.J. Kennedy
All rights reserved.
Manufactured in the United States of America.

Library of Congress Cataloging in Publication Data

Moore, Richard, 1927-
    Empires.

    (Ontario Review Press poetry series)
    I. Title   II. Series.
PS3563.063E4   811'.54   81-82505
ISBN 0-86538-013-9   AACR2
ISBN 0-86538-014-7 (pbk.)

Distributed by PERSEA BOOKS, Inc.
225 Lafayette Street
New York, N.Y. 10012

For
Warren Leamon

PREFACE

AMERICAN poets are continually trying to leap out of their skins. Generally, at the moment, this leap ends with the poet looking out of the eyeholes of something mindless or inanimate: a bear or a thundercloud, a newt or a worm, a tree or a stone. (A brief peruse through a sheaf of recent poetry journals will turn up a great number of such poems.) It is much less common in American poetry at the moment for a poet to make an imaginative leap into an interesting human mind. In *Empires*, Richard Moore projects his intelligence and sensibility into a quartet of the remarkable dead, who unburden themselves in memorable cadences.

Only first-rate poets, I believe, have been attracted to write such demanding monologues: Tennyson and Browning, and in recent times Pound and Lowell. To attempt such a difficult enterprise is characteristic of Moore. He has never cared to write an expected sort of poem, whatever that is; all along, he has written poetry according to his inner light, his irascible quirks, and his ever clear and feelingful reason. One can expect of him only a stab at the supposedly impossible—whether in his successful attempt at a contemporary sonnet sequence (in *Word from the Hills*, University of Georgia Press, 1972), or his achievement of an immense satiric epic whose protagonist is a mouse (to be published in 1982 by The Countryman Press). *Empires* is another astonishing feat, in which Moore resoundingly does exactly what he sets himself to do.

Which is—? Among other aims, Moore sets out to establish a colossal metaphor in setting ancient Rome and expansionist America side by side. The four celebrated speakers—Aaron Burr, Jay Gould, Archimedes, and (yes!) Cleopatra—are persons in whose hands enormous power has lain, and who (in various degrees) have been equally the victims of it. Gould, whose part in the Black Friday panic earned him the epithet "most hated man in America," is a perfect exemplar—being left in the end with tunnel vision of his own doom, and that of his family. Though Gould has manipulated great wealth without concern for its effect on people, he is himself not diabolical—he remarks, at one tranquil moment in his career, that he "entertained some thoughts of honesty." In bringing to life Archimedes, Moore (himself a devout mathematician) portrays a man not quite the lover of abstract beauty we have imagined: a more human being than he who, absorbed in drawing circles in the sand, could hardly find time to die. Archimedes, as Moore shows him, has seen his intellectual labors serve the cause of war; and in this, he becomes as contemporary for us as any biological researcher whose work suddenly is coveted by the Pentagon.

It is Moore's art to make these lives impinge on ours. (The vivacity of his Cleopatra has to be read to be believed.) This immense four-part poem (incidentally, cast in fittingly various and flexible blank verse) keeps the poet's vow: that he will invent no fact unnecessarily. But where he does invent, as you'll find, he invents spectacularly well.

X. J. KENNEDY

CONTENTS

BURR

Enter the traitor, villain of his Age,
ready to consummate his villainy
on an old whore, belle of our Colonies,
fresh-minted States. Jefferson, Hamilton,
dead coiners both, you can't attend; you'd gloat.
Yes, it's a shoddy business; but she's rich.
My debts require the lady more than I,
near eighty now, still hot and competent,
the tiny man with fierceness in his eyes.

Yet it will end badly, as everything
I've done—heroics at Quebec, brave deeds
to salt our General's bunglings in New York,
then Valley Forge, where the rough mutineers,
freezing in rags and sick of discipline,
came at me with the rifles I'd unloaded.
I let their leader aim and squeeze his trigger
then with my sabre neatly sliced his arm off.
Martinet Burr had triumphed, and in style—
a gory elegance uniquely his.
The great whiskery muzzle of the Army
learned that the cat had claws—yelped and was silent.
And yet their sufferings drained all my fortune.
In sleepless wizardries I broke my health,
having brought order to Connecticut.
Washington kindly let me leave, a pauper.

Dull George, needing some brilliance at his side,
chose Hamilton, the bastard, who'd have reasons,
permanent motives for obedience.
A bastard's bastardizing lasts forever,
seldom degenerates to independence.
It's like a Negro's blackness in our South.
But I'm unkind to George: no man's all dull
who knows he's dull, and he exhibited
the planter's instinct for the proper slave.

My troubles began there; grandfather Edwards,
you of the subtle mind and frenzied pulpit,
Jonathan, George could smell you in my blood—
or else ancestral pride of German princes,
trickling through a Princeton president
into this orphan—sirs, your humble servant.
I'm told George was afraid I read his letters.
Indeed I did—victimized by that urge,
sweet to the light of heart, to play magician:
I find longevity's their sole reward.
But always when I faced friends or opponents,
beautiful machinations, artistries,
harmless but unexpected, kept them guessing.
If that is villainy, then call me villain.
And who discovered Howe's first battle plan?

Then we were lawyers, Hamilton and I,
the legal giants of New York, fine young
resident geniuses before the Bar.
His grand oceans of rhetoric could swell,
well and inundate opposition, plunging
them deep in weighty, stately matters. I,
master of technicalities, could pull
plugs from the bathtubs where they floated. O,
Hamilton was a man of principle:
firmly believed the rich should remain rich,
the solid bulwarks of our warlike State,
where some are bulwarks, others die in war.
I can agree it's pleasant to be rich:
the sanctity eludes me. Sarpedon
in Homer knows that true nobility,
the right to sit in honor at the feast,
ought to depend on fearlessness in battle.
The Sarpedon in Homer died at Troy.

Solemn pretensions of our landed rich
sickened me. I supported Jefferson.
How else could I beleaguer Hamilton,
who, having married himself wealthy, felt
all wealth as holy as his matrimony—
counter his dull Barbados counting house
philosophy with mischief—good bright mischief?

We had no bank. No Democrat could get
loans; Hamilton could pass on every tradesman;
and as we starved, the City lacked good water,
and only Burr detected the relation.
Clear a water company was needed.
Under their noses, Burr's fine print included,
it passed—that water company—and lo!
it was a bank, and Burr was its director.
Partisans, gathering around me, cried,
shame! shame! as the bank layed its waterpipes.
The only shame they found was being tricked.
That was the only shame they ever found,
Hamilton, Jefferson, and all the others.

The loopholes I could find were for the people
to clamber through. They were the needle's eye
camels and rich men have no need of. Then,
citizens needed property to vote,
and vote they did—as many as a hundred
co-owners of a single house—whereby
we overthrew elections, Federalists,
captured New York, the pivot State, and Burr
became dangerous to our institutions,
creating with his rabble Presidents.

I never visited their halls myself,
belonging as I did among the rich—
master of legal nuance, speculator,

fantastic juggler of prodigious debts,
and in that happy mansion on the Hudson
host to ambassadors—I, who had married,
to the astonishment of all, not wealth,
nor great beauty, but one I could delight in.
Beautiful women danced round everywhere,
and others not so beautiful—no matter—
they too—I had my little weaknesses,
monstrous in frequency and crowed about
by the quilled hacks Hamilton kept in pay—
but she, that widow stranded with two sons,
yet with such spirit and such gaiety,
though darks nibbled already that destroyed her. . . .
Women possess a brilliance all their own—
everything filtered through another light,
books, knowledge, the arts, all in a strange glow,
as if their first tones, wild and whimsical,
had spoken. I was mad for education—
to bring that female light into the open;
and she, dying, had left me with a daughter,
my Theodosia, my high delight.
Everyone knows how brilliantly she shined,
my sweet creation. Best reason for life,
how could I bother being President
when to that grandest wedding of the time
you went amarrying in Albany?

For Jefferson and I had won at last,
he with philosophy and I with votes,
won equally: the Congress must decide.
Indeed, he was the Party's head, to which
somewhat mischievously I'd been attached,
one of the brawny legs that made it stand.
It was a loophole in our new-made System
that tied our votes, and Burr, expert in loopholes,
easily might have triumphed, had he tried.

The Country was in turmoil, Federalists
anxious for Burr instead of Jefferson.
Hamilton, hating Jefferson, wrote letters,
finding it in his heart to hate me more:
Jefferson's principles were dangerous,
but they were principles; and what had Burr,
that selfish man, but glory, pride, and debts?
Woman-corruptor, vile, unscrupulous,
and vilest of all, Hamilton's gadfly.

And yet, despite his letter-writing frenzies,
his Federalists approached me. Jefferson,
also approached, gave sweet assurances,
while Burr was silent, the unscrupulous.
Having no principles to compromise
he stayed in Albany and drank champagne
while Jefferson told every Federalist
in Washington he meant no revolution;
but still the long deadlock meandered on
through ballot after ballot in the House,
Jefferson further from the goal than I.
I drank; my bags were packed; but I said nothing.

Jefferson won. Absurd and perverse pride—
the same that never let me answer slanders,
until the false filth clinging to my name
helped Jefferson smell out a gallows for me. . . .
Can daughters' marriages be so unhinging?
Or were there promptings in me that the Land
belonged to Jefferson, and to his snout,
sniffing out every public prejudice,
until a voice within cried, Let him have it?

And now, near eighty, I can see at last
I'm a poor judge of character. I think
too well of people, and they don't forgive me.

Jefferson's Vice-President, I was ruined.
Powerless office...when he looked at me,
he felt no joy: but for the grace of Burr,
Burr would have been the monarch in his place.
Could Thomas Jefferson feel gratitude?
My ground crumbled; there were no offices
for the poor fools who had supported me.
Jefferson saw to all; nothing remained
beneath me now. A faint tap, and I'd tumble
into the maws of creditors below.

Practical politicians, if you're brilliant,
hide it; and if you cannot hide your brilliance,
comfort the people with the sweet conviction
you've drained it into harmless principles,
empty philosophies, crack-pated theories.
Good revolutionary—Jefferson,
who've since become our stately deity—
rebel—as long as property's protected—
what good you did in office violated
your own theories, and everything from theory—
that mad embargo—was catastrophe.
Your pious harping on the Rights of Man
with scarce a word about the state of slaves
mocked the perceptions of the simplest child.
We'll suffer for these quaint hypocrisies—
suffer already in our silent hearts,
where unadmitted lies breed agony.
Burr got the slaves their freedom in New York,
Burr first, and not from any principle:
mean practicality, low common sense
declared it decent, sensible, and just.
The beggars might have felt, say, gratitude—
seeing I didn't make them Presidents.

"Life, Liberty, and the pursuit," you wrote,
"of happiness." Happiness? Jefferson,
you should have left it reading, "property."
Cross out "happiness." "Property" was honest.
O, but it wasn't ringing; it was low.
Safer to make the sentence meaningless.
How can a Nation gather and be founded
without grand-sounding words? When low men lead,
how can they tell the truth? And so the Myth
of the Republic blunders fondly on,
till the compacted lies on which it rolls
crumble to sand and leave us derelict,
obliged to contemplate ourselves at last.

So Burr presided four years in the Senate,
known for his just, if testy, discipline.
In all effects, my useful life was over.
They'd cast me—or I'd cast myself—as nothing:
a weird nonsense, a public negative,
a vacuum, symbolizing God knew what,
that dashed about the States, tornadolike,
attracting flotsam, jetsam to my center.

Near my term's end, now ripe to be replaced
by a dim, doddering non-entity,
I stopped to snuff out Hamilton at last,
who, wildly fearful lest I might become
Governor of New York, outdid himself,
forgot his caution, let his name be used,
and—filled with dreams of playing Bonaparte
when once Burr's rabble rose and ruined all—
took up my challenge to preserve his good
repute for courage, military genius.
He claimed he disapproved of duelling,
wrote privately he'd shoot into clear air
above me; met me, took good aim, and missed.

Duels, of course, were customary then,
but just this once, for the Vice-President,
murder indictments were arranged. I traveled
more widely now than ever—till once more
Jefferson needed me, this time to try
the Supreme Court in chambers of the Senate,
poor Justice Chase to represent his kind
and play sinner before the White House God.
Burr with his flair for panoply and style
was just made for a solemn farce like that.
Chase was acquitted, Jefferson chagrined.
No one denied my fairness in the matter
or that I might have won my master's favor.

O yes indeed, governments must be solemn;
yet without humor, where's solemnity,
where's noble ritual? It is a game,
my friends, played with a duelist's precision:
you need a touch of lofty irony
and laughter in your heart to do it right.
But they, upholders of our dignity,
munching their apples on the Senate floor,
dealing in greasy waistcoats with the State,
cried shame because I dared magnificence,
loved women, laughed in money-lender's faces,
and was at home with Old World subtleties.
O, the conclusion's obvious: not man,
no, money is the measure of all things.

And yet I almost conquered Mexico
and ended life a home-grown emperor
with rabble out of forest settlements
down the Ohio floating to adventure,
who'd flocked to nothing more than Burr's repute.
The Land was waiting, ready for brave actions—
canals to be run, river rapids tamed;

tracts to be settled in Louisiana,
deeded and in my pocket; Mexico
sheer vacancy: what marvels might have flared,
had a mere band of men danced in that void,
that crumbling mansion of the Spanish Empire?

Out of my shrinking near to nothingness,
gladness of battles. . . . That night long ago
when sudden cannon fire at Quebec
blasted the whole front rank, but left me standing—
commander and men gone, only the boy
untouched, who sensed his moment come and called,
Forward!—and on to take the city, take
untakable Quebec!—and we'd have done it,
had not an elder duffer from the rear,
in sudden terror of those emptied cannon
and technically commander now, cried out,
Retreat!—and the great game was lost forever:
that night, I think, accounts for Aaron Burr.
Battle-enduring has a fine effect:
we're either killed or feel invincible.

After my years in the starched, peaceful East,
the West had such a swagger—such receptions—
mad noble Irishmen on river islands
with gorgeous wives to please my traveled daughter,
whose husband poured us money out of Georgia.
Jackson, of future fame, a happy puppy
wagging his tail, turned out the frontier towns—
dances and balls for celebrated Burr,
who'd met and killed his man. O lovely bubbles,
scampering down the muddy tides of State!

From the beginning, there was talk of treason.
Our States had trickled westward through the mountains
that walled them from the inner Continent,

but the new land, filling with pioneers,
touched on an old world reaching back to Spain.
Those ridges seemed to saw our Land in two:
the new part, washed by rivers to the Gulf,
could deal directly with the powers of Europe
and so become a nation on its own—
and who better to lead it now than Burr?
Absurdities!—fit for the empty fears
of the stuffed statesmen in the Capitol.
Out there, you heard the home-state dialects
and each man name relatives in the East.

But still I jested. The woods worked with rumors,
attracting riflemen to shiny nothings,
all phrased so delicately, hintingly,
no one was sure exactly what I'd told him.
A single man can't stir up a rebellion,
which, if it happens, happens of itself.
The pleasure of it was the gleeful thought
of Jefferson alarmed, fearing the worst,
filling the absent woods with messengers,
his chops watering for the scraps of news.
Burr moved, and half the West was touched with wonder,
busily organizing trials that proved
nothing—mere supposition, likelihood
and Burr remained incomprehensible.

Jefferson had his way of stirring passions,
and I had mine. Though both of us told lies,
mine spun no webs of sickly sentiment;
mine recognized a man and duped him plainly;
once he could listen better, he'd be free.

And so we requisitioned pork and beans,
bullets and muskets, from astonished merchants,
and Blennerhassett's beautiful estate

was wrecked by law-enlisted ruffians.
But in New Orleans sworn friends attended.
All was in motion, creeping down the rivers.
The mad adventure well might have succeeded,
but for my greatest co-conspirator,
a large, flatulent General of the Army,
high in the confidence of Jefferson
and Spain—Spain, too—I smile to think of it.
This fat rascal was Jefferson's star witness
against me later, so incompetent
the high court tittered with embarrassment.
Under him all Louisiana waited
tensely in arms and plundered by his rule,
as the dread scourge, the devil Burr, approached
on six old flatboats stuffed with trusty yokels.
The only man of interest to the General,
I fled before he had his chance to hang me,
was caught eastward and brought to Washington—
to Richmond, rather—Jefferson's Virginia.

Our monarch there, with his respect for law,
for Life, Liberty, and the Rights of Man,
by the authority of his high office
proclaimed me a known traitor through the Land
and, confident no jury'd dare acquit me,
brought me to trial. Excitement swamped all hearts,
and the town hummed with hempy expectation.

Poor Jefferson, he seemed to float so high,
until the plug was pulled. He had forgotten
that even primed juries need evidence
and that the judge (the Supreme Court's John Marshall,
a man of honesty) can be required
to judge its relevance. That eager jury
returned, mournful and angry, with the verdict:
the known treason of Burr had not been proved.

Ah, what were my deep motives, after all?
I loathe your undertakings with results
patly predictable. Give me some doubts
and a gay splash of possibilities.
Think what you will, but ask: what was the clearest
witness of Jefferson's hypocrisy?
Where does it shine more for the world to see
than in the farcical conspiracy
and shameful trial of Aaron Burr? The proof
demonstrable: the man's manifest lust
not only to undo me, but to hang me.

Something bemonsters our rough populace
that must express itself with Jeffersons
and Hamiltons and scuttle simple justice,
drowning all men in principles and parties.
Let's say that our new Constitution found us
both cats and dogs, people unreconciled
as to their future character; why then,
after my trial the matter stood decided:
henceforth, in parties all, we'd be dogs only.
Look there at Jefferson and Hamilton—
they're dead—look at their portraits, if you will—
notice that shaggy dog-look in their eyes,
a certain vague, eager expectancy—
no gemlike swiftness to the kill: their food
comes from subservience—to thoughts, to causes—
our city spaniel and our country sheep-dog,
our thoroughbreds. Mongrels come frisking after,
claiming descent. They're all frightened of cats.

Now the whole Country clamors, Mexico!
and traitors' plans inspire patriots,
and so the dogs will howl. . . . As for your cats,
they clean themselves, follow their inclinations,
never ingratiate themselves to men,

nor climb to offices above their natures.
They never snap at beggars at the door
nor bark at order in the universe.
They kill, as creatures must, but when they purr,
women and children willingly adore them.

Where's one to sniff out sweet enlightenment?
I was an ordinary selfish man;
I can conceive of better ones; but let
them live submitted, not to principles,
but to particulars—each separate case
a lovely world, revolving on its own,
its own intricacies, its own delights.
Your principles bring on hypocrisies
that falsify the fool who would believe
along with the contriver who deludes.
Who needs those priests to tell us right from wrong?
They with their litanies would rule our thoughts,
bereave us of our natures—and for what?
The tribe? The priests? The sanctity of God?
The vanity of Thomas Jefferson?
O, let our plain self-interest rule, whereby
we're not degraded into less than men
through vain desires to be more than men!
Let us have decency and appetite—
for when our native decency is gone,
appetite, too, will wither in our hearts.

But now all sweets were over—the house sold
where the ambassadors could feel at home.
Thinkers and scientists, wits, poets, rogues,
must find out other havens now, the men
whose individualities I loved,
aided, and in particular, one rare,
excellent artist, whom I helped to fame,
glimpsed in his fame when I was destitute

in Paris—there's your topsy-turviness,
your madcap wild indifference of the fates—
my farthings gone on women as I starved,
teasing that nightmare-maker, Bonaparte,
with trifling reveries of Mexico.

Received in England, lionized in Sweden,
in Germany a plaything for the princes,
sipping the fountains of my ancient wrath:
five brilliant days in Weimar at the Court.
Goethe delighted in me, glad, he said,
one man on earth had glimpsed its comedy.
Cling, he advised me, to my images,
hold tight to Mexico, because, he said,
only absurdities deserve belief.
That helped me past a Baroness's snares—
the sorceress—the one woman I fled,
down all my corridors of life, in terror.

But when the women had soaked up the farthings
and still no navy led to Mexico,
why, though a Baroness had beckoned me—
O why my perverse longing to go home
to filthy creditors and enemies
and men frightened because they'd been my friends?
I had a daughter still, and she a son.
It wasn't easy, then, to visualize
ways for the blood of Burr to dwindle more.
I had to sell the thousand gifts I'd brought them
to get my shabby self upon their shores,
resolved to settle for a dreary age,
if only they were near me once again.
I found my countrymen would let me live,
took up the musty ends of practice, then
found how resourcefully Burr's blood could shrink still.
Her son stricken with fever in the South—

yet Theodosia was still alive,
would be near soon—a cutter up the coast—
so easy, easy—it's a legend still—
ship, sails, girl, swallowed up in nothingness,
the empty, fruitless tossing of the waves,
and nothing more for us—yet there I stood,
ready to go on unmolested now.

Good future times, do not dismiss me, saying,
"Burr was a sordid little man." That's not
enough. Burr had a grandeur in his actions
this sniveling Republic will do ill
without. A high comedy thrived in him
that was the clearest mirror of its time.
A healthy State lives in its mischief making,
sprouts wisdom from its saucy negatives.
Good future times, bother with your opinion.
It will consist of lies in any case,
and I have graver business now: to die—
only light-hearted souls know how to die—
properly. Humdrum years, but now—adventure.
There is an ancient lady waiting for me,
a noted whore when we were Colonies,
a speculating beauty in her lushness.
Her independence was a foppish merchant
grown rich, escaping Jefferson's embargo—
but this old widow he did not escape.
On, therefore, to the lady and my last
absurdity, one last wild raucous scheme
that sets the whole town jabbering once more. . . .
And then deep quiet, looking down the Hudson. . . .
That boat brings Theodosia to me.

GOULD

Tuberculosis bleeds this millionaire—
disease of poets, unrequited lovers—
spits out America's most hated man,
anguish of rival speculators, rage
of journalists, scandal of ministers. . . .
Sweet children, I had soft poetic eyes,
unknown before, they say, in financiers,
dark and intense. When you looked into them
you felt sympathy, understanding for you,
dreams; and you never guessed, until too late,
the nightmares waiting for you there behind them,
that left you spent and writhing. Hooks of greed. . .
but for the greed of others, I'd be poor.
I made Black Friday for them: gold itself,
the tender root and spinal of the Nation,
twitched to the tune I squeaked, the mousy recluse.
And President and Treasury danced too,
till all rioted, screaming for my blood
in their despair, panicked like spirits damned,
while I sat tearing papers in a room,
quietly milking millions from their madness.
Beautiful Fisk was caught, but him I saved.

You gather there, my children, my lost loves,
around me in this touching bedroom scene
and watch my waxen face and try to hear
each labored and faint breath, but cannot hear
these echoes now, beyond my sunken eyes.
I've taken leave of each, each servant also,
Gould in his house, kind memory to all,
press of his cold hand, whisper from his lips,
and now these quiet hours, the last long silence,
the words with which I lull myself to death.
You worry me, my children, more than thoughts
I entertain of life beyond this bed.
What if my empire tumbles ruin on you,

pampered like helpless princelings of a court?
You never drove the cows home for your father,
who wished the weakling stronger, healthier,
less useless, less the darling of his sisters;
never were child clerks who could see just how
America rewards the weak and honest—
disease, starvation, husks for the poorhouse.
Is there a greater sin than poverty?
Why are the poor, then, so despicable?

And so the ticker ticks quotations still
in the next room, and all is well with prices.
Wall Street is calm. Although it knows Jay Gould
wastes here, my corporations do not waver.
Will they stay steady, children, when I'm dead?
Will my ghost gaze and think the risks well taken?

People will deal in chance. Your minister,
doctor, and barber all love speculation.
(Haven't I said that, somewhere back in life?)
Laws against gambling would promote it merely.
Why, business, children, is like life itself.
Your perfect speculator, perfect gambler,
like an unborn spirit among the stars,
intuits when to enter, when stay out,
and most important, when to leave, once in.
I hear the ticker, ticking out my fate.
O the procedure, children, the procedure!
We need not hesitate about *dimensions*!

Go into anything promising profit.
Wall Street is like an ocean, full of eddies,
currents. . . . I fear a storm for you, a shipwreck.
Haven't I also in vivacious times
beaten it to a froth and whistled spray
in every speculator's eye? Behold:

they sowed the wind and wept, reaping my whirlwind.
"This Erie war," said Vanderbilt, "has taught me
never to kick a skunk." And on his deathbed
that violent uncouth man, who could cheat
his own son for the joy and could commit
the wife insane who had endured him years
because she didn't like a house he'd built,
declared that skunk the master of the game.

Erie began my empire, rusty rails
fatal to workers, cattle, passengers,
daily derailments, fires, and monthly wrecks,
plundered by financiers before I came,
by pious Daniel Drew, who sucked its blood
until he thought its skin and bones were worthless.
Young Fisk, who'd lost three purses in the market,
charmed the old codger with his roaring tales,
but needed more than charm, needed the wits
found sometimes in your mousy types. . . . Old men—
old sentimental fathers whom I gulled,
climbing from nothing to a modest fortune,
Pratt who was hurt, and Leupp who shot himself,
and Drew who, stripped by me, died penniless—
little boy Fisk I loved: fat, full of swagger,
vulgar with puns and plump effrontery,
a gaudy circus of a man, whose paunch
lusted for mistresses but could beget
nothing. His impotence, his tipsy song—
thrills of a hairless boy in empty bushes.

We throve; Vanderbilt saw and thought he'd conquer,
own all the railroads in New York, and charge
passengers, freight, exactly what he pleased.
He bought shares; and our basement printing press
each night printed more shares for him to buy.
Four millions poorer, he awoke and found

Erie afloat still in our watered stock.
Then when he called his hired judges out,
we packed suitcases of his money, paddled
most of a foggy night across the Hudson,
and Vanderbilt awoke once more and found
Erie incorporated in New Jersey.

Taylor's hotel there boomed with us, where Fisk
marshalled his mistresses and Drew in terror
sniveled about his bodyguards and saw
in every shadow thugs from Vanderbilt
sent to abscond with his frail bones to justice.
We watched him closely. Drew was treacherous.
Jersey police in squads came to protect us,
leaving the other streets so clear for thieves
there was a sudden crimewave in the city;
and Fisk took charge, our military genius,
puffing Perfectos on the prowl, back-slapping,
serving the troops good whiskey by the keg.
Him, he proclaimed, they'd never take alive,
him the defender of the poorer classes
against the vile New York monopolist.

Vanderbilt tried Albany next and paid
the legislature to illegalize
our stock. Again I packed bags of his money,
and in those marble halls that never flowed
so with a raging flood of bribes before
or since, I bought the legislature back.

Even our Vanderbilt's strong belly turned
sick with disgust at that, and "Skunks!" he cried,
and Wall Street laughed to see its Titan beaten.
I sped in triumph back to our madhouse
to find Drew with our treasury escaped,
gone bleating overtures to Vanderbilt.

That fixed his fate, bad-breathed hypocrite,
rubbing his Bible while he lied and swindled,
sly old drover who'd fed his cattle salt
and fattened cows on water for the market.
He'd wanted to endow a seminary;
he'd only wanted to enjoy his millions—
as if a thing like that were possible.
Only the getting of them gives us joy—
taking what others want, connive and fight for.
O children, be content with merely spending.

I knew a trick to get the treasure back,
and we all made peace. Drew and Vanderbilt
got cash and Fisk and I the rusty rails
and the deep printing press that paid our bills;
and I, a young man in my early thirties,
my tricks hidden behind a thick black beard,
voted myself the railroad's president,
elephant Fisk its managing director,
and we become the image of the age.

Those were the days when Tweed began his rule
and every city office went on sale.
He joined the board, and law was on our side.
The press clattered; our capital stock doubled
in four months, and the price of Erie shares
jumped up or fell, a puppet on our strings;
and Drew was caught. He went to law; the judge
was Tweed's; and Wall Street giggled with delight.
And Drew, shut on the outside now, exclaimed,
"This is like buying cows by candlelight,"
and then, "Beware of Gould. His touch is death,"
and four years later died and left a watch
and two old hymnbooks to posterity.

That was the year our Erie grew to grandeur.
We bought and moved to the Grand Opera House
so Fisk could feel at home with divas, dancers,
two ballet troupes, one blond and one brunette,
all for his whim, and Erie paid for all—
for Mrs. Mansfield and her house nearby,
her services a thousand dollars monthly,
the regiment he bought, to be its colonel,
the ships he owned, to be their admiral.
He played, and the whole town, excited, watched—
because, I think, he managed to express
with such a sumptuous vulgarity
secret imaginings in every man.
Christ, preachers tell us, suffered for us all;
Jim Fisk, like some lost Pharaoh of the Nile,
orgied, caroused, and pleasured for us all.
Your starving clerk could dream of Mr. Fisk,
admiral, colonel, uniforms aglow.
We other robbers, drab, black-suited men,
were trunk and branch; Fisk was the gorgeous flower.
And since he made the whole game seem worthwhile,
he was good business too—until the wind
shriveled him loose and dropped him in a gutter.

Meanwhile a bolder scheme than all that tinsel
was working in my mind: to corner gold,
buy all the gold there was with bogus checks,
create a false demand, drive up the price,
and, while all speculated on its rise,
sell every ounce of it I owned and make
eleven million dollars in a morning.
Bribes would be needed, so the Government
wouldn't sell gold to stabilize the price.
President Grant, unwittingly I'm told,
took part: his sister's husband was a rascal
carefully cultivated by us both.

Fisk was reluctant, couldn't understand
beauties like these—that Grant need hesitate
days only, hours, while the panic grew
and chaos bloomed and paralyzed the Country.

I needed Fisk there on the Gold Exchange,
shouldering hugely through the frenzied crowd,
his great voice buying, booming up the price—
and also had to sacrifice him there,
keeping him buying while I sold in secret,
keeping the news a secret when I heard
that in an hour the Government would sell.
We found a way, though, to untangle him,
renounced his debts, stayed locked in "Castle Erie,"
our Opera House, our singing offices,
while process servers stormed its bolted gates
and gangs we'd hired rallied to protect us.
Fisk could appreciate me, understand
he was a puppet on my fingers, danced,
jiggled, and flourished in my calculations.

His end came, not from me, but Mrs. Mansfield:
Ned Stokes' bullet, who, her latest lover,
had hoped that Fisk would go on paying her.
Fisk wrecked his business. Mrs. Mansfield then
offered some old love letters for a price.
Our lawyers stripped and drove them in a corner—
and Ned came out, most unexpectedly....
No bullets could be found in so much fat
when doctors probed in Fisk's enormous belly.
It felt, he told us, like the sour apples
he ate too many of, as a boy once—
as a boy, said it—and his wife forgave him—
while I sat sobbing in the corridor...
and all relish was suddenly extinct.

O children, after some small youthful tricks
to leave the farm and get a start in life,
and after happy marriage to your mother,
I entertained some thoughts of honesty,
till Fisk called forth the genius that was in me.
After he left me in that corridor,
success followed success, mechanically
almost, although my audience was gone.
Railroads pried open the enormous West—
expansion everywhere, and everywhere
corruption, corporations to be plundered.
Gould flitted batlike on the Nation's vision—
so frail and quiet, such a gentle person.

People compared me to the traitor, Burr,
who once foxed the Republic in the West
and died obscure the year that I was born.
Was I—are we—some strange degeneration?
Is there an order possible in life
that would permit a boldness in our actions
without exciting such opprobrium?

Being precocious, what had I to fear?
After I wrote a history and sold it,
surveyed two counties, drew, and sold the maps,
and not yet twenty, had a stake in life,
wasn't I safe enough from poverty?
Why did I cheat an old man of his faith,
honor, and eighty thousand dollars? Pratt
having a weakness and that tender boy
such brains, ambition, and soft brooding eyes . . .
what powers are in us? What does a young man
do with his queer itch for supremacy?
What measures his success but earthly men?
Let him be poor, honest; they'll claim they love him.
Forgive me, children, I preferred their hate.

I've heard they whispered Gould was a Jew. No,
we're flowers, darlings, of America.
My father, farmer though he was, drew blood
from proud Connecticut aristocrats:
Puritan Bradleys, Talcotts, Burrs enough
to serve your haughty Astors, Vanderbilts,
and Morgans, one and all, who sniff and shut
you out. The Vanderbilts are proud perhaps
that their progenitor, eager for profit,
once put a Union force to sea in hulks
so rotten that the nails dropped from their timbers;
and maybe Morgan celebrates the time
he sold the Army old discarded rifles
and, though they blew men's thumbs off, got his payment.
And I avoided military service;
there were no heroes that way, only fools.
Seeing that young men for a modest sum
could purchase pardon from the battlefield,
I left the dying to the sturdy poor
and rigged a telegraph by which I knew
before the market how the battles went:
defeat, victory—profits were the same.

And yet my profits maimed no Union soldiers.
Nor have I probed, like Morgan, other countries,
buying up this and that from simpletons
too innocent to realize what they own,
and when they learn, asked Congress to protect me.
We need those markets for stability,
he says. We'll need a bigger army too.
In this the Southerners deserve some praise,
who wanted outright slaves and honest conquest
and scorned this Northern pussyfooting empire.

Where's any joy in snuffing out the helpless?
Give me professionals, good competition,

smart men greedy as I. I never plundered
a corporation that had not been well
plundered already, and I never gave
profound justifications for my thefts
nor tried to wipe them clean with pieties.
For that, no minister can pardon me.

And dear God, save me from your Cyrus Fields,
your grand developers, your noble builders!
To think it helps the mind and health of men
to lay a cable underneath an ocean
so continents can lie to one another.
Save me from the pitiful divided men,
their pure desire for wealth and social status
corrupted by the urge to do good works.

Ask of my workers whom the rails make happy.
They are paid nothing, squeezed and starved and maimed. . . .
This child labor, this grinding down of men,
misery manufactured in the mass—
well, is it worse than misery on farms
that scattered piecemeal through the countryside
and through the squalid centuries unchanged?
Only, we see it now. They see it too.
And if men's pains are ultimately mental,
what of the sudden strangeness of their lives
in stone-faced cities with capricious laws,
where families break, relationships decay,
and crazed fathers blast their bewildered children?
God's cosmos was a giant watch, we said,
and God its watchmaker. Now see the dream
in rails and engines actual at last
and men ground squirming in its lifeless wheels.

Why would I marvel, therefore, that they'd riot?
Why would I feel a pang, crushing their riots?

What, would I show kindness and yield a place
for purer Goulds more ruthless than myself
to crush me? Always in our histories
when there's a certain way of doing things,
one man arises to epitomize it.
The game had to be played, and the self-righteous,
seeing me demonstrate its rules, were shocked.
Every monstrosity shall reach perfection.
That was my greatest service, my lost children,
to be the lonely brilliant one, the essence
of the great scheme with no redeeming joys
in wine or women, and the one that all
others less brilliant, less successful, less
open, but no less greedy and corrupt,
could point at, shouting, monster! thereby gaining
ease for their consciences, salve for their envy.

Here in my last thin hour above the ground
shall I dig up the root of my success,
my dears? What could supply me poise to know,
unclouded by my own fears and desires,
what other men would do, so I could trap them?
What but in some bare corner of my mind
to feel a numbness, sense a sick detachment?
Control, perception flourish in detachment.
No one who's desperate to win wins much.

There on the Gold Exchange, shredding my paper,
a nervous nothing in the hub of things,
the empty calm inside that hurricane. . . .
between this whispered devil of Wall Street,
and one whom children, wife, and servants loved,
did something grow in silence, blossoming,
worm through my hours of reading every night?
I think the mathematics that I mastered
when young to get surveying in my grasp

unfolded graces that I relished more
than poor Jim Fisk champagne and dancing girls.

I loved my orchids and my formal gardens,
old books, but most the quiet of the night.
Sometimes I'd contemplate a spot
upon the wall or title on the shelves
whose gilt dissolved in such delicious bliss,
fully aware, the whole room emptiness,
not even dark—a gray without dimension. . . .
Then I'd come back with the new problem solved,
the next bold act miraculously clear.
Erie and gold, Union Pacific wars,
Manhattan diddled of its precious rails,
the Vanderbilts turned out of Western Union.
Each time the wolves howled for my wasting flesh.
O had those orchids nothing else to say?

My books, Mark Twain, Sir Walter Scott, and Dickens,
authors who would have hated what I was,
and histories that told how such as I
age after age lay heavy on each land.
Is there no other order possible?
We'll multiply our laws, enact controls,
but Goulds will rise and master any system,
until all systems crumble into ruin.
Aren't merest savages more fortunate
who win themselves prominence in the tribe,
setting their traps merely for animals
or snaring spirits in a frenzied dance?
I had the finest orchids in the world,
azaleas, blooms from the deepest jungles,
and tended them in quiet ecstasy.

How did the boy become a monster? Pratt,
the first step on my long intricate climb,

leaving retirement to be my partner
—my work, his money—in a tannery,
I knew would come one day to find out why
with the production up and markets good
that tannery produced so little profit.
He'd find the books confusing, needlessly
complex, would hear about my private bank,
swelling with unaccountable deposits.
I, in New York, arranging other backing,
returned to find him, troubled and indignant,
looking intently, asking me the meaning.

"No meaning, sir. I've only cheated you."

This man who'd loved me as a father might
looked in my eyes, saw glassy insolence
and all their depths of boyish admiration
annulled, and stood there, dumb; and I believe
that sad old gentleman produced a tear.
I knew, knew he could never prosecute!
I knew, therefore, he'd try to catch me short,
demand money, insist I buy him out,
and in New York that day I'd made arrangements.
And when he said he'd have his partner's half,
he was surprised again: I took his offer,
didn't break down, repenting as expected.
He got back half his capital—just that:
I kept the other half and the fat profits.
My New York backer was a man named Leupp,
another honored and respected merchant
who'd kept the old traditions, fond beliefs.
He found me charming, learned my ways of dealing,
and that year fired a bullet through his brain.

And there's another secret too for those
who bring forth nothing, only lie and swindle:

master all inner promptings, strangle all
sweet spontaneities, and let no laughter
tickle and flick up corners of your mouth.
In all my life I only uttered once
an honest word in public. On Black Friday
a man in ruin cried he'd see the day
I'd have to make my living in the street,
cranking an organ, begging with a monkey.
"Maybe you will," I said, "maybe you will;
and when I want a monkey, George, I'll send
for you." Why cause the poor man added anguish?
To cheat him of his cheatings was enough.

No, nothing was enough, and all was empty.
Gould batlike, vermin fitted out with wings,
darting uncannily about our twilight;
Gould mouselike in his labyrinth of wealth—
five hundred acres on the lower Hudson
castled and landscaped, guards at every gate,
my bomb-proofed offices in Western Union,
my private railway car, whose locomotive
fired me twice a year around the Nation—
neuralgia clawing me, insomnia,
and for my stomach, crackers and warm milk—
and still fresh scheming twitched my wasting body,
until I paced it nightly, coughing blood,
in the dim street with one lone bodyguard,
sleep and my lost Union Pacific still
eluding me. . . all things eluding me.

I milked this grandeur from my father's cows.
How easily one takes the spring for granted
and the bare earth denuded of the snow—
shriveled decay of autumn everywhere,
tatters that cumber the fresh blades and shoots.
Dead wife, you lie on me like broken leaves.

Torn by the specter of my dealings—all
my improprieties—what stopped your heart,
the speculators ruined, workers crushed,
or George, our first son, married to an actress?
You feared our Helen destined for a coachman.
I kissed, indulged them. Whims were all they had.

Daughter of merchants, Murray Hill traditions,
proud of your duties, management of houses,
six children born, raised, guarded from kidnappers,
what did you make of it, the daily tread
of the police outside the house, the fear
of robbers, lunatics, extortionists,
the men turned violent whom I had ruined,
the anarchists our ways of life enraged?
Cruises aboard the *Atalanta*, manned
in blue and white, the livery of Gould,
on sundrenched southern seas all failed to heal you,
relax your slowly tensing arteries....

And in this bed my flesh shall never leave,
my long descent, darker and still more dark,
ledgers of corporations in my mind
broken and torn and flaking in the wind
that blows forever through the darkness. Still
I hear the ticker, ticking like a heart,
and know now it will mock my day of death,
and all my stocks, as if in joy, will rise,
from Gould's great jungle orchids free at last;
and now, protected children, I can see
already your disordered, aimless lives,
caught in this subtle labyrinth I made.
Children, to whom I showed all gentleness,
hoping to spare, you also I have ruined.

ARCHIMEDES

In a way, yes, it's monstrous what I do—
tickle these whims, these nothings, into proofs,
these beautiful clear pictures in the mind.
Figures I scribe and contemplate in sand
are not the sand and not my markings in it,
which only represent them. What are they?
The skeleton of things that our sharp thoughts
probe and display. Here, sirs, pick at these bones.
A point is that which has no magnitude,
that is, is nothingness. But let it travel
and trace that heightened nothingness, a line;
let the line move and generate a plane,
then hoop the plane into a cone, a sphere,
then bring on Archimedes, who will solve
all riddles. I shall have them on my grave:
a sphere inscribed within a cylinder,
because I first detected their relation.
Through all the ages since the world began,
the sphere and cylinder related so,
but no one knew, there was no mind to see it;
then Archimedes lived, and he has seen it,
and put it shining in the light of day,
where it will stay for all ages to come,
perhaps.
    Romans are grunting at the gates,
and soon the gates must buckle, soon the sword
flash in my study, nick what necks it finds. . . .
Engines of Archimedes, deep in thought—
catapults, winches, winging balls of fire—
maimed and bewildered them through three dark years
but it was futile, and the neck is old
with hardly blood enough to stain a sword.

And now there's one last problem to be solved.
First, how to meet Marcellus when he comes,
their general, who has me in his thoughts;

and next, how close the circle of my years
to leave the central point of me defined.
Two questions, but I think they are related. . . .
Seventy years is long enough to live,
I hear a young man say. But I am old.
Gelon, my beauty, I have seen you die,
you and your father, king of Syracuse,
who made an edict for my sake, and told
the city: now in everything he says
mad Archimedes is to be believed.

"Mad as his father, the astronomer,"
giggled the women and the dirty workmen
who saw me running naked from the bath,
shouting, "I've found it, found it," through the streets.

"Give me a lever and a place to stand,"
I said one night, "and I will move the earth."
King Hiero laughed and offered me more wine.
But the next day I rigged ratchets and spools,
and Hiero pumped a lever with one hand,
and from the harbor inched his greatest ship,
laden with cargo, out on squealing gravel.
He offered wine again and made his edict.

Of course, merely to drag a ship on land,
a work slaves will accomplish as before,
was not our aim—our aims were never low—
but to display the power of the mind
over those things it has no need to touch.
The work that's worthy, men will do themselves;
and work that's menial, they leave to slaves;
but to perform a labor by machine
voids it of life and meaning altogether.

Those sunny days of wisdom in our state
are gone now, gone King Hiero and his son,
his grandson murdered by the mob that shrieked
vengeance on Rome, and all his progeny
wiped out. Romans besieged these walls before;
young Hiero, born between a slave girl's thighs
and king of us because he'd won our battles,
acknowledged error, made his peace with Rome,
and fifty golden years rewarded us.

One only had to see how Carthage dwindled.
But Epicydes and Hypocrates
were blind. Marcellus ordered: Throw them out.
We made them generals instead. Of whom?
Of Greeks? Greeks hire their spearmen nowadays
and hope they'll die and not prove treacherous.
Old Hiero's death unleashed those Carthage-lovers.
Why, Hannibal had Italy in flames!
At Nola who stopped Hannibal? Marcellus.
Enough. These thoughts prove nothing that I need.

Like catapults, our politics are shadows
cast by a clearer form within the mind.
I think that form is mathematical
and is the point which has no magnitude
that is the center of our civil life,
the fountain of our arts and our corruption.

We picture magnitudes divorced from things;
children do not, nor women hardly, nor
do tribes, I think, that roam the growling hills.
Yet all make drawings, dances, poetry.
In all our new magnificence of cities
only this number-subtlety is new.
Note how our words for numbers lack inflections,
unchanging strangers in our sentences.

To own things men must count them; when they count,
they speculate and loosen from those things—
from herds, from earth pregnant with seeds and spirits;
loosen from ignorance and innocence;
and as their theorems grow, so do their cities;
and money is invented and corruption,
and everything is numbered and for sale.

O Alexandria, you show the way
with dregs from every sea collected in you,
with Ptolemies, who've never seen that Nile
that loads their noisy palaces with gold,
and with your famous university,
your mammoth marble haunt of all the Muses
where Conon showed me excellence of mind
and brought me up that Nile which lies beyond—
whose pyramids, intricate waterworks,
nourish more men than anywhere on earth.
I made a clever pump that helped the peasants . . .
only came home at last to Syracuse
to ease my maddened father to his grave.
A simple man, he measured sun and moon,
or tried to . . . till the moon riddled his brain.

Still, still the pure form grows, rounds to the full
in reasoning that glitters like a god
and rides the night, pretending to depend
only upon agreement with itself.
Indeed a pretense: paradoxes lurk
in every proof for those who care to see.
For who can prove our premises correct,
consistent, independent of each other?
All rests on acquiescence, on the old
daily perceptions of the things about us
and the old darknesses within us, whence
discoveries are born. But where's the seed?

Plato, who stayed in Syracuse before
my days, marked mathematics as the pole
on which the tent, philosophy, was hung,
that keeps our spirits dry in every rain.
I wish the word-lovers who comb his thoughts
for fleas of meaning would remember that.
But did he understand geometry?
I wonder. Demonstrations are the meat
and sauce the Socrates he pictured serves
to all those docile little answerers
who troop like shadows through his dialogues—
as if our hair and hearts were geometric!
Poets are mad, he said. Theocritus,
my dear dead friend, was rational enough.
Contrast Empedocles, who boiled in Aetna,
riddled with philosophic speculations.
Ah, Plato, there's a madness that inspires
even our intricate geometries,
and many lovely theorems come to light
out of the low mechanics you despised.
When we define a straight line as the shortest
distance between two points, sometimes I think:
Nonsense; a straight line is a string drawn taut
between two nails. Tighten it, Plato, feel
that unused distance ooze between your fingers.
Think how we solved the cone and pyramid.
In the last age Eudoxus found the proofs,
amazing proofs of what was long surmised.
Then would you give Democritus no praise
for boldly speaking what he'd only guessed?
What put that saucy fancy in his brain?
Some lordly instinct leads us to these things—
as cats to little morsels in the night.

Then praise the old crazy Phythagoreans,
who knew such mysteries for what they were

and are no longer. Mysteries have died,
secrets emerge into the light of day,
and scholars think the sun will always shine. . . .
Ah, will my soul transmigrate into others,
as they have said, throughout millenniums?
Crazy, and yet they found the twelve-faced solid:
the cube with squares turned into pentagons
and doubled to accommodate each other
yet regular and perfect as a cube.
I say that all our careful subtleties
will never catch the boldness of that find.
We prove; who formed the notion of a proof?
O, do they seem ridiculous to us?
Well then, let's all be laughable as they.

One needs the touch of laughter to conceive
new things—one needs the wildness of the grove. . .
By *novae res,* "new things," the Romans mean
in their tongue revolution in the State;
and if they unify our fickle cities
under their laws, there'll be no new things more.
Sweet gods, they've the solemnity to do it.
Has it been done in other worlds than ours,
as the Pythagoreans might have said?
In Egypt there have been no new things now
what bleak millenniums? They are well fed
and live, as slaves do, under stable rule
with drunken Ptolemies to roam their void.

I think my father lacked that depth of laughter,
that tipsiness that sometimes tips the world
with all the stars into an unguessed order—
and makes the ground totter on which we stand.
Something was much too timid in his soul,
for all his madness, all his mad devotion.
He laughed, but never at astronomy,

disliked the poets, never glanced at earth—
great shoulders slumped, brows pinched into a scowl
brooding the nights through, till the stars he dreamed
went dark, lost in his rectitude of art.
And then the rage, the strictures in his blood. . . .
And as for me, I've left his stars in peace—
and once I proved to Gelon there's a number
greater than all the counted grains of sand
if sand filled up the star-thick universe.
Ah father, did I stuff your stars with earth?
Or did I empty them into a thought?

The town was awed that knew I sat whole days
as in a trance, neglecting food and drink,
my bath, my bed, forgetting wife and slaves,
slave to the subtle shapes inside my mind;
but was that godlike pose the total figure?
Once when they broke in, hauled me to the bath,
the water rising, pushed up round my body,
showed me the very thought that I'd groped for.
The meditation readied me for that—
the stillness they had seen, the hub of me:
around it, plunging heaviness of mind
sinks down into the muddy earth and clings,
and that's the rim that bears the chariot,
splendid in sunlight, murderous in war.

A storm of fire bursting from the walls
surprised the Roman Legions come by land
and lashed them down the slopes of Epipolae.
Gigantic mirrors round the harborside
made Syracuse so flash with sudden suns
confusion shouted in the Roman ships,
where flecks of flaming pitch rained, splashing fire.
Some say my mirrors burned that Roman fleet.
Let them imagine: I imagine too.

But all the horrors my machines achieved
couldn't preserve a city bent by men
blind as those walls I'd made impregnable.
A drunken festival of Artemis
opened them, and our soldiers' treachery.
Now only this high quarter on the harbor
holds. Storm gathers, and the streets are quiet.
There's hunger; there is nothing more to sell.
The ships of Carthage all have sailed away.
Romans or adverse winds deflect the cargoes
come to supply us, if indeed they come,
for there's no profit in us any more.

Power of Carthage—does it have a center?
A great family or two, that's all they have,
mere traders, uninspired copiers.
Do their admirers love their taste in art,
literature? What are they famous for:
justice—or cushions, beds, and mattresses?
With engineering of the Greeks they mix
Egyptian magic, stars of Babylon,
and Tannith, goddess of abominations,
who drinks the blood of children every spring.
They've made great voyages round Africa,
reached to unheard-of islands in the North,
and Hannibal's still loose in Italy.
Carthage, your every boldness stinks of commerce.
Are Romans any better in their greed?

Romans revere our thought and are our fate.
They mold their clumsy language to our styles,
and though they cannot feel geometry
deeply enough to add a single proof,
they know their outward works are from its forms
and sense that men have symmetries within them.
He spoils his symmetry who reaches out

to finger distant corners of the earth.
There's meat enough for gluttony at home.
He spoils his clarity and manly poise
whose blood is drawn by the irrational.
Civilization is the work of men,
not women....
              Yet mad Archimedes relished
women, embraced those thoughtless savages.
Didn't this thoughtless body in the bath
buoy up my thoughts into an unguessed science?
Something that has no being in the mind
glitters in wayward eyes, in dreams, in angers....

Hear Archimedes, crazy as a woman!
Here at my end and sinking of my city
I cling to earth tenaciously as they.
The problem still, the problem! On my grave
a cone and sphere inside a cylinder....
One simple measurement defines them all;
no earthly number ever can define
their volumes, that in ratios forever
recede from us in inexactitude;
and yet those volumes there beyond our grasp,
contained in the cone, sphere, and cylinder,
are to each other as one, two, and three.
This I have proved incontrovertibly.

The gods recede in inexactitude.
Where else but in my nothings do we find
certainty, truth? Languages fray and fade;
poets grow meaningless and are forgotten;
but Archimedes' theorems are eternal—
embalm our very spirits.
              And the merchants
will find a use for them. Hamil of Carthage
asked me to make our numbers more convenient

so every fool can calculate with ease,
producing answers as by slight of hand,
by rule, by rote, like jugglers in a circus,
or like Egyptians plodding through the mud.
Sirs, I have shown you proofs where all stands clear,
as does a statue to caressing eyes,
in steps, inventions, and constructions that
the gods themselves would find incredible—
yet not one calculation to confuse:
all plain in words, lines, simple ratios.
My Greeks, play out these possibilities;
such proofs may not exist again on earth.

Where are the numbers Ancient Egypt found?
Who'd understand them, Ptolemies or slaves?. . .
Our cities grow, plundering countrysides.
Will their soil fail?. . . Along the endless Nile
the ruins crumble like forgotten theorems. . . .
We freed ourselves; Pull down the oligarchs,
we cried; better to let the people rule.
But now the people lose their sense of rule,
and swords have come to hack them back to rule.

He'll send for me; he is a cultured man.
I'll be the learned monkey at his triumph.
And when they triumph in all cities, all
wisdom will be as monkeys in a circus.

We see those petals falling from the stem,
but who has guessed what roots are shriveling
and what will be when every god's been emptied?
People will write their poems, play their flutes,
dance; but the excellent discoveries
we made will cease abruptly when complete.
In all those shapes there's not one living thing.

I was the greatest of geometers,
a mere savage mechanic loosed in thought.
What is this itch to know the rule of things
and follow logic to its flaming end?
In triumphs of the mind we were as gods
who can escape all touch, all pain, all life.
What are these numbers but oblivion?
What were our cities but the sand that boys
shape to their dreams and nightmares by the shore
where centuries like tides wash them to nothing?

The gates cave in; blood raining in the streets;
men groan there, bleeding; screams of women fastened,
and children gently fettered for the market.
There'll be an angry soldier in my study,
angry to have this labor, fetch this dry
old man, balding and shriveled, from this chair,
while all his fellows rush in blood and plunder.
"By order of Marcellus, come!" he grunts.

"Do not disturb me, sir; I contemplate."

"Come to our general, I say!". . . All still.

I've seen the short patience of bloody men.
He raises his nicked sword. "Look up, old man!"
Only my silence, and it maddens him . . . .

Indeed it was ourselves that we discovered
in forms we felt in things, their order, poise.
And when the life's complete, the corpse remains.
It's clear now. I bequeath my corpse to Rome.

IN ROME

Enthroned with Caesar, monarchs of the earth—
that would have been so suitable for me,
the sun's daughter, the sister of the moon.
No one believes that in this upstart city
of stucco huts and drafty little villas.
City of Alexander on my Nile,
splendor and pleasure of the earth, must you
be ruled by sons of shepherds and their goats?
Caesar detests them quite as much as I—
dotes on them too, and that will be our ruin.
O, I am certain the exciting fate
that he conceived in me will come to nothing
and Cleopatra sticks in Rome in vain.

More than a year! The Ides of March again.
I must consider . . . in two days he sails . . .
the Ides—fate's balance of the day and night.
I'll hold rituals lofty and mysterious!
No one disturbs me, knowing that I scatter
deaths like unwanted garments when displeased.
Leave me in peace, I told them, though you hear
Caesar himself were murdered in the Senate.

They say I'm not the beauty I'm reputed—
my skin too darkly golden, nose too sharp.
So say the Roman women. But the men?
Well, I have wit and know some things by heart.
Didn't I tickle Caesar's failing powers
until that hot old epileptic got
a child in me? He's nearly three now,
Ptolemy Caesar, and may yet become
Pharaoh of Egypt and this dying world.
For that I love old Caesar, for his wits,
boldness—and for I think he is a god.

But I must pray to Mother Isis, Cypris,
Diana, every goddess who will come,
and think a little while, as thinkers do,
and let these Romans sift down into me,
open myself to them until they tell
which of them will protect me and my son—
because I'm certain Caesar longs for death,
and men wait ready to fulfill his wish,
and what they bungle, archers will accomplish:
in two days he departs for Parthia,
if he's not murdered first. Then I to Egypt;
and neither, I am certain, shall return.

These Roman women all are politicians,
legal and philosophical as men;
but lacking the appendages of men,
they're impotent, they have no proper natures,
callous and brittle, though they rock the world.
They think I am too young to be a queen,
too small and frivolous to be so haughty;
dislike my coiled luxuriance of hair
differently tied and shaped each time they see it;
distrust the smile that wholly fills my face,
the eyes that see exactly what they look at,
darkly alight, released from fear and dreams.
They say we women of the clever Greeks
are savages. Indeed, we savages
may know things Roman matrons have forgotten.
Cypris, you've told me things beneath the moon;
maybe this morning you will speak again.

The pleasures and the mysteries of life
have always come so easily to me,
ease in my body's boyish suppleness,
ease on the tongue that speaks eight languages
and can enchant men's ears with melody,

ease in my skipping thoughts that seem to wear
as careless curls or laughter in my speech
the darkest, richest kingdom of the earth.

Yes, but my girlish years were not so easy
among the muffled sounds of family murders.
My little father, Ptolemy, "The Piper,"
who fluted sad sobriety away
between his banquets, orgies, poisonings,
and anxious trips to Rome to bribe the Senate,
murdered my sister to regain his throne.
His formal title, "Neos Dionysos,"
commemorates his taste in love and wine.
What wit we had in names we gave ourselves!
Old Philopater, "Lover of his Father,"
murdered his father to assume that title.
Some said we Ptolemies were decadent
and half Egyptian after all these years.
I helped Caesar perceive that we were brilliant
and proper creatures of a dynasty
that had survived in peace for centuries,
while the free cities hacked themselves to pieces.
Though we were gory cats among ourselves,
wasn't our Alexandria the most
magnificent creation of the Greeks?
Were we not patrons of the arts? And though
the arts have died, I am their patron still.

We learned from the Egyptians, but our secret
was Alexander's, who first taught the Greeks
empire and oriental ways of power:
deification of the murderers
and madmen in the palace. Rome, how else
can your prim sons of liberty be ruled?. . .
What are those laws by which they claim they govern?
Tricks written for the rich and powerful

to gloss and misinterpret as they please—
I'll never understand them, I confess.
People need love, hate, something personal
to show the hope and hopelessness of life
unwearied by this drab pretense of justice.

Poor father—he was illegitimate
and all his life contended with the will
made by his predecessor, leaving all
his property to Rome. Fortunately
the Senate hardly dared accept a gift
surpassing in its wealth, if not its power
—my people being peaceable and happy—
great Rome itself and all its provinces.
Whom would they dare appoint its governor?
How could he hold my gay Egyptians, who
require a god or goddess as their ruler?
O, they'd have made that governor divine
and sent him back in gold and silks to Rome,
whence he'd return, the folds of his fine robes
crawling with eager greedy senators,
and thus great Rome would vanish into Egypt.
So father bribed his kingdom year to year
and payed off Caesar's debts and Pompey's friends.

I was a girl of eighteen when he died
just seven years ago, his eldest child
born of a wife of whom we need not speak,
with brothers and a sister to destroy
before my throne could be secure. Three years
passed, and my brother's eunuch seized the Palace,
missed me with poison, and in Syria
a girl became the general of an army.

But as that little Ptolemy and I
faced one another in our desert camps

along the shore from our gay capital,
Pompey arrived, after Pharsalia,
the great battle that lost the world to Caesar—
for any Roman looks for help in Egypt,
defeated or victorious. For losers, we're
the last big independent kingdom left;
for winners, we're a huge necessity.
Because my people fill the world with grain
that financiers of Alexandria
can transmute into splendor, ships, and gold,
no Roman with a need to pay an army
ever ignores our helplessness for long.

Even my brother's eunuch was confused
at Pompey anchored there, waiting, who'd been
the strongest friend of Ptolemies in Rome.
To harbor him would surely anger Caesar;
to send him off make him an enemy.
So from his galley in a little skiff
they landed him, and while his anxious wife watched,
they hacked his handsome head off—and the galley,
wailing, spread canvas seaward.
                                    Some days later,
Caesar arrived, and leaving us encamped,
stationed two legions on the Palace walls
and made himself at home. Romans were there
already, still collecting father's bribes
directly from the Palace revenues,
so Caesar's presence had a certain pretext.
My brother sped to him with Pompey's head,
which Caesar took rather ungraciously,
weeping, and summoned all our house before him.

How could I go, with bright brotherly daggers
waiting at each dark corner of the way?
But then one afternoon a peddler Greek,

calling himself Apollodorus, paddled
his dory to the Palace docks, announced
he'd property of Rome, rolled in his rug,
and once admitted to the Palace, cried,
"Bring me to Caesar, I've a gift for him
that he will value much." Caesar appeared;
Apollodorus laid the carpet down;
and out rolled Cleopatra, Queen of Egypt,
babbling Latin with a charming accent.

Caesar enjoyed the trick, and liked my looks,
and that I was a queen did not displease him,
this dapper balding perfumed little man
who had seduced numerous queens already—
to say nothing of kings from time to time,
although his days of lechery were waning.

Next day he called my brother in, read father's
will, and suggested reconciliation.
My brother sensed his doom being prepared,
threw down his crown, dashed from the room in tears,
and then a nasty little war began.

Against Caesar's desires, my brother's army
had stayed intact and occupied the City;
and now it seems his eunuch had in secret
armed the Egyptian fleet in the great harbor.
Caesar, who had no men to man a fleet,
set it afire. The Great Library burned,
and no scholar can guess how many scrolls
of lies and folly perished in the flames.
Next he attacked great Pharos Light, that marble
marvel that climbs skyward five hundred feet
and shines glittering white by day and with
a lamp at night quite forty miles to sea
and guides ships from all corners of the world

to plunder Egypt—took it, and secured
free passage to his provinces beyond.

Other exciting incidents occurred
while Caesar unconcerned laughed through the nights,
royally entertained himself by day,
surprised at how it felt to be a monarch.
My little sister fled, hoping to be
the queen—for which she later marched in chains
in Rome at Caesar's triumph; and that eunuch,
caught at his poisons, was at last beheaded.
There was a thrilling battle on the causeway
between the harbors, that sent Caesar swimming,
holding his papers up to keep them dry,
dragging his scarlet cloak between his teeth,
and ducking spears and arrows aimed at him.
Four hundred legionnaires went down that day,
who couldn't swim. But reinforcements came—
at last armies from Syria, we heard;
and I conceived a charming stratagem.
According to the Alexandrians,
they fought to free their king, held by the Romans,
whose life indeed was inconvenient to us.
We gave him up, as if we wished for peace,
then with him there among the enemy,
we fought the final battle, where he fell,
drowned in his golden corselet in the Nile.

I see his tears, pleading to stay with us.
You don't keep dynasties with tears and pity.
That left me one small brother more, and he
was easily disposed of two years later.

Six months had passed, and I was growing plump
with Caesar's heir. Rome had appointed him
dictator for the year: as well to let

love that the people felt for Pompey fade
before he entered Rome and staged his triumphs;
and meanwhile Egypt fascinated him—
the thirty thousand towns beyond the Delta
that neither he nor I had ever seen,
although I spoke the language, was the first
Ptolemy ruler to have troubled with it—
vast fields richer than Romans can imagine:
three crops a year out of the Nile's dark mud
spread wide through sluices, locks, and waterways,
organized by the priests, all property
of Amon-Ra, God of the sun, and of
the Queen, his representative on earth.

All we could see of this were loads of grain
pouring across the Mareotic Lake.
And there was trade from India as well:
a new route slowly growing famous, new
delicacies in Alexandria
unknown in Rome, silks, gems, exciting spices.
It went by sea around the Parthians
and down the Nile and was a better route
to India than Alexander marched.
Casear, whom Alexander haunted, heard
and dreamed of armies where the merchants went.

So we we took ship and voyaged up the Nile
aboard my thalamegos with its gardens,
its colonnaded courts, its thousand oars,
southward upstream into the desert winds.
Always on either side the barren cliffs
closed in the river and the magic valley
cluttered with ruins to the roots of time.
Four hundred boats of soldiers went with us.
Caesar was aiming for the Nile's far reaches—
but turned back at the first cataract's thunder

merely because his legionnaires were grumpy,
grumbled about the labor and the heat.
I was astonished then and have been since
what little obstacles could change his course.

Yet, as it was, the journey filled my time.
In Alexandria, back in the cool
sweet breezes of the world, a son was born,
a goddess for his mother, for his father
Amon, who had appeared on earth as Caesar.
Yet he refused to be anointed Pharaoh.
He was afraid what this dull Rome would say
merely because he had a wife already,
merely because his Romans hated kings.
Didn't he rule Rome and the broken world?
What other man on earth had such an army?
I should have realized then that all our plans
to hold the world together were a dream
Caesar himself would make impossible.

Banqueting in the Palace through the war
and on the Nile before my child was born,
he had declared two clear alternatives.
He could depose me, make my endless Nile
his private property, and purchase Rome;
or he could keep me as his queen and found
what Rome would shortly need in any case:
a dynasty with oriental pomp,
deified rulers, orgies, poisonings. . . .
Something inside him failed at such a thought,
so foreign to the grudging senators
he had manipulated all his life
and to the scarred soldiers who followed him.
And yet to rule Egyptians by himself,
he'd have to be their god, or they'd revolt,
ruin their waterworks, and starve the world.

That's what he needs his Cleopatra for:
confidence in his role and in its wisdom.
There will, I think, be no more sons for Caesar,
or if there are, there'll be no queen to bear them.
What other queen could tickle him as I do?

I came to Rome, therefore, to view his triumphs,
observe my younger sister march in chains,
and show Romans the Queen was quite unconquered.
We set about our plans for monarchy:
a throne of gold for Caesar in the Senate,
his statue placed among the ancient kings,
image among the gods at festivals;
and when with reeking dinners for the crowds
his new temple of Venus Genetrix,
the goddess that his clan's descended from,
was opened, there, as goddess in the sanctum,
the Queen of Egypt carved in marble stood,
and the loud crowd shouted approval of it.
What if a few fool senators were silent?

And yet how vexed and hectic Caesar seemed,
as if those senators had poisoned him,
his slight, emaciated body taut,
his gestures quick, eyes with a wilder glitter—
so fascinated with his plans and powers,
as if distracted. In this Circus world
of mock battles where gladiators bleed,
where Cicero collects old furniture
and translates Plato into homilies,
nothing is real; though everything is Greek,
they keep of Greeks only their arrogance.
Men spun such beautiful philosophies
for five mad centuries. But now it's dead,
the beauty; and an ugliness lives on
in Rome, a numbed rigidity of mind

that is the strength, perhaps, of conquerors
but bane of those they conquer and themselves.
In any kingdom one expects some sly
corruption; only Romans are corrupt
on principle, proclaim with moral fervor
the rights of citizens, which means the right
of senators to plunder provinces.
Greeks can at least remember their pretense
that godly decencies could move a city.
In Rome, founded by bandits, vagabonds,
and slaves a mere few hundred years ago,
they only grasp the usefulness of pretense
to keep the people cowed and armies marching,
and ignorant what decencies might be,
they hawk and hem and venerate their vices.
And have these lies they live on made them strong?
Their plain incompetence amazes me.
Caesar's in need of my astronomers
to give Romans a proper calendar,
requires my coiners to improve his mints,
my clerks and financiers to organize
his treasury. These conquerors are helpless.

And now whatever strength they might have had
is crushed under the burdens of their conquests.
The times are right for Caesar; earlier,
he might have been a villain in the State,
a renowned traitor, lost in comedy.
Always his nonchalance astonished me,
thriving on opportunities and chances—
scarcely a thought of overall direction,
the broad sweep of the river through the wastes.
For all his victories, when he appeared,
he struck me as a leaf, driven in wind,
that has no notion of the tree, where leaves
grow and have purpose—of trunk, branches, roots

that have endured in brute stolidity
longer than leaves or than the lives of men.
Wasn't our Alexander much the same
for whom being a god was like a madness?

In frills of kingship, he turns arrogant
and all the little villas hum with scandal.
He angered senators by staying seated
when they had come to bring him honors,
and, like a child, tantrummed because a Tribune
once in the Senate failed to rise for him.
Why shouldn't he be so? To win his battles,
conquer so much, yet go on risking all,
didn't he know himself beneath the moon
divine? Wasn't he undefeatable?
Since his worst flatterers speak proven fact,
he is obliged to breathe in every word.
A god can sniff up flattery and thrive;
in man the fibres of the heart decay.
Is he surprised at this? Doesn't he know
that rulers of the world need to be mad,
expressing, as they do, the world? Thrust up
as on a pyramid's gilt pinnacle,
far from the little labors of the earth,
nothing to touch him but the sunlit air,
he withers. Oedipus before his death
becomes a god, grows arrogant and rages.
As Sophocles portrayed, so Caesar does.

Is it too much after the battles won
and years campaigning through the world
to ask him to take up once more the old
cynical politicking of his youth?
More than a year I've watched him give offense
and grow exhausted, climbing up to godhead;
and now he still showers poor wincing Rome

with edicts pouring daily from his pen,
as if he'd change Italy in a year
or make it grow to hate him, which it has.
Plans to divert the Tiber from its course,
dig a canal to please Corinthians,
a great new road across the Apennines,
new temples, new harbor at Ostia,
casual statements that his government
ought to be more convenient in the world,
in Alexandria, Byzantium,
or Troy—something to think about when crowned,
but to drop hints about it now is folly.
Caesar, you must conciliate and flatter. . . .

But the mood's changed, and all hangs on the mood.
The pudgy Ciceros and sons of Cato
have had their chance to talk and write their letters
and undermine the grand effects of Caesar—
while he who makes them angry pardons them.

A month ago the Lupercalia,
reinstituted and reorganized
to make it like the festival in Egypt
with Lupercus, god of fertility,
portrayed by wrinkled Caesar on a throne,
was held, and as the agent of the god,
Antony, brilliant in his nudity,
went dashing, lashing with his jackal thongs
the women he could find in every street—
for thus old Lupercus would make them pregnant.
Then at the end, all glittering with sweat,
he ran to Caesar and presented him
a laurel crown. Beautifully staged it was
with agents hired to start cheers in the crowd.
But the crowd moaned; and Caesar put the crown
aside. At that the crowd broke into cheers.

Thus Rome is ruled; the rabble's absolute.
Caesar, you pulled this down upon yourself
with your irresolution, awe of custom,
and doddering disunity of purpose,
fearing the very thing we know you longed for.

Old man, I think you shrivel on the branch.
It's time I thought of others to protect me,
young and corrupt as I, who know the world
needs kings...queens.
                              Gods, what have we here but Romans?
Antony, Brutus, and Octavian—
playboy, philosopher, and sickly nephew
whom Caesar's designated as his heir
because there's still no dynasty in Rome:
upon these three, I think, the earth depends,
and I as well, since I am but the earth.

Brutus, all maxims, pithy axioms,
Pythagoreans, Stoics, and the rest,
who chews on ancient Roman principles
as goats on dung...these abstract men are deadly.
I'm sure he'd kill his mother if he thought
Plato approved—and feel proud of himself
for having overcome animal terrors
and low unreasoned pieties to do it.
My spies all say he leads the latest plot,
now Antony's been reconciled to Caesar,
hopes to resuscitate the dead Republic
and trick it out in fresh legalities.
All Rome but Caesar knows—who will not listen.
"What, do you think Brutus will not wait out
the time appointed for this little body,
thinking it quick and soft as yours, dear queen?"
he jested when I told him all I knew—
had pardoned Brutus, since he'd fought for Pompey

not greedily, but out of deep belief.
O Caesar, surely that was cause to kill one
certain to be your enemy forever.
Was it because you thought Brutus your son
got in another's wife, who was so lewd
it is impossible to guess his father?
Brutus detests your blithe solicitude
and says stiffly his father was her husband.
To think you thought of him as your successor!
And what will Brutus do when Caesar's dead?
Can such a man behave politically?
Cypris, the notion's inconceivable.
The first wild demagogic speech by some
drunkard will sweep him to oblivion.

Octavian believes in nothing, not
himself, not the Republic, not this life.
He is a dead thing, pimpled, ill at ease,
and sly; has lusts that are disgusting, kills
coldly and for the pleasure, when he dares.
He'd be the one to play both god in Egypt
and hypocrite in Rome—the one who won't
need me. . . .
            Let me have Antony, who's gay,
plays tricks, pretends he's Bacchus in his wine,
and charms even the dull women of Rome.
Bring me his tedious vulgarity;
maybe this clown who can command, lead battles,
suffer, will play a proper role sometime.

No one can play the role that Caesar plays
or make the monarchy that he'd have made.
O Caesar, Caesar, you must stay alive!
Two weeks ago—these last Calends of March—
he planned it in the Senate. Rumors barked
he'd be assassinated on the spot,

and he drew back. And now the Ides have come.
There's talk they'll make him king at last today—
relishing Parthia no more than I,
that taxes their estates to pay his armies. . . .
Or will they sever all his schemes with knives?

The only way to achieve kingship now,
he says, is conquest of the Parthians.
Gods! he's been planning that for a whole year,
and days before he leaves he finds that reason.
What will be changed if Parthia's subdued?
Will Cicero like Cleopatra more
when more monarchs in chains limp down the streets?
He thinks battles will free his soul from Rome
and lapses into old familiar ways. . .
and pardons all: are poisons out of date?—
and lets them speak: there'll be no peace in Rome
until some senators contribute blood.

The days are passing like a troubled dream.
There'll be no Parthian campaign, no conquest
of India down Alexander's path,
and no return for Caesar through the gates
in triumph, crowned and deified at last.
Rome's not fated to conquer Parthia.
Thinkers and scholars, do your intellects
demand preciser reasons than I give?
Then hear: Parthia's much too big and wild,
too full of bows and arrows, cavalry,
and rocky wastes that pay an army poorly.
That, Crassus found, whom Parthians extinguished
in witty honor of his Roman greed
by pouring gold they'd melted down his throat.
Romans can plunder people like themselves,
Greeks, Gauls, Spaniards, or Macedonians;
Egyptians are too rich and Parthians

too poor. Witty, cries Caesar, and he laughs—
for he still has his gaiety about him—
and then a shadow falls across his face
because my nonsense is the simple truth,
which he must hide, as one hides death . . . . He knows
he has become too frail to take the field
for three arduous years, too old, too mad.
Haggard with epilepsy and his dreams,
Caesar's like Rome: a ruin rules the world.

He'll die as Alexander, far from home.
A gloom hangs on the City; ghostly lights
flicker about the midnight sky, and shapes
of horror have been seen, monstrosities;
rioting breaks out daily in the Forum.
He dined last night with Marcus Lepidus;
the party asked what kind of death were best:
"A sudden one!" he cried, as though he felt
the quick dagger release his weary limbs
and relished it. He's gloomy—or he laughs
and says, "I'm Caesar; I am no mere king!"
O Caesar, be content: kingship would come.
Do not seek death to prove you are a god.
We have a happy god in Egypt who
can live, play music, drink at festivals . . . .
Who screamed? I told them . . .
                            Caesar? Murdered? Words!
Didn't I tell them? Blood will . . . has it happened?
Then what's that wail out there, for me to hear?
They daren't disturb me, but they dare do that—
and footsteps shuffling beyond the doors
and—murdered . . . slaughtered . . . .
                            Quiet now. They're gone.
It's gone. Our Monarchy a pool of blood,
the plotters fleeing from the bleeding corpse . . . .

He was no god to drink at festivals.
He had no taste for wine, nor for fine foods.
O Caesar, Caesar, why did you dismiss,
as if in scorn, your Spanish bodyguards
who followed you through every colonnade?
Why did you laugh at me and take no heed?
And now you have your death, but what have I,
fed by that cynical enthusiasm
that was the flavor of the gods in men?

He was as water rushing among rocks
that one can see in his wild Apennines,
downward and downward, finding every cleft
and splashing through it swiftly, carelessly,
turning this way and that, responding always
to the land's shape, to fissures, crevices,
with no direction but the silent depths,
motionless sea, the final quietness of Empire.

Has Rome, then, murdered him, who brought it peace?
And if it will accept at last the gift
I bring, will it, then, also murder me?
Cypris, I feel your prophecy upon me
and hear your laughter echo in my throat.
There will be wars again: a war to sweep
Brutus beneath the earth; then Parthia
shall be invaded, and catastrophe
follow Rome's ruined armies once again;
then civil wars, as Rome in cries of pain
brings forth its monster monarchy at last.
But Cleopatra's name an infamy
and sordid joke among the continents;
and your name, Caesar, sacred; but your son
hunted above the cataracts and drowned.

Still there is Egypt, always silent Egypt. . . .
And in the stillness of the summer nights
when torches shone across the deep lagoon
and there was revelry, and drums and flutes
mingled with lights, heaving upon the water,
the wharves in labor, songs of fishermen. . . .
Out of my people came the gaiety
of Pharaohs. All are leaves now on that tree
whose seed was planted in the depths of time.
Then let Octavian pronounce the Empire
and make Egypt his own private estate.
Egypt will conquer him and all his people;
and Alexandria shall rule in Rome
in fashion, artistry, and in corruption,
just as his wife shall rule Octavian
with poisonings and children for his lusts.
But Cleopatra will not march in chains
to decorate the Roman's empty triumph,
for there's a needle always in my hair
hollowed and filled with poison, and a snake
that crawls in mud and reeds beside the Nile
that gives a painless and a rapid death,
and there's a peasant who will bring that snake
to me, because his people live forever
and I in agony became their Queen.

AFTERWORD

WHAT is one to make of one's past? The question has two meanings (How is one to understand one's past? and, How is one to exploit and transform it in order to make something new?) and they mingle. For there can be no understanding without such re-creation, such more-or-less blatant storytelling and myth-making. (To understand anything is to find—create—a pattern in it.) And there can be no such myth-making without distortion. To understand one's past, one must be willing to misunderstand it. We would like to believe that we are simply collecting data and that the collection, if we can only make it big enough, complete enough, will speak for itself. That's the worst myth of all. The books get larger and larger and mean less and less. The collections will never speak. Only human beings can speak. Or gods.

A dear friend of mine will put nothing into his historical novels that is not officially known to have taken place. No one living today knows—in the manner that historians know things—where Cleopatra was when Julius Caesar was assassinated. She might have been in Rome or she might already have returned to Alexandria. My friend would have had to contrive some way—some wonderfully ingenious way—to be noncommittal about her whereabouts at that moment. He insists that this is the only way to be fair with the facts. It seems to me that he is being overscrupulous with them rather—and at the cost of being unfair to the story, to our need to understand and misunderstand. For stories have an overwhelming tendency to know where their characters are: here or there and rarely at sea in between.

On the other hand, there is an arrogance sometimes: a willingness to wring history's neck, so to speak, in order to make it squawk what one already has in mind. I am thinking of Thornton Wilder's fascinating transformation of Julius Caesar into a kind of Nietzschean superman. That recorded facts have been changed in the story is not crucial, but it is symptomatic: one feels that the writer in the intensity of his own purpose did not care who or what Caesar was. Caesar was deified. He was a god. He could have spoken to Wilder. But would Wilder have listened?

My ideal has been to submit the imagination to history: to the fact of it and to the story and coherence of it. Many coherences are possible. Shakespeare's Cleopatra was beautifully accurate to the spirit and fact of the historical record in his day, which consisted largely of Plutarch and some fruitful misunderstandings of Plutarch. The facts of the record are different now; and the spirit—*a* spirit—has to be rediscovered.

The germ of this book (if it is like a disease)—or the irritating bit of grit lost at its center (if it is like a pearl)—was a remark in Theodore Morrison's history of the United States that Burr's conspiracy was an absurdity, a bit of *opera buffa* in the wilderness. (I hope I quote the Admiral correctly.) Our dreadful Aaron Burr? Comedy is the drum to which I march, the flag that beckons me onwards into whatever horrors await; so I went to the library for a book on Burr. I was lucky: a huge modern study was out at the time, and I came back with an older book, sparser in facts, written by a man with a florid style and a passionate conviction that Burr had been maligned by history. As I read, humor sprouted everywhere. It was a good thing to happen to a man who puts Moliere and Sophocles on the same pedestal.

But it was a bad experience for my wife. She felt that I was turning into Burr, that her husband was being inhabited by a ghost. I didn't know who I was, nor did I fret much about it. Things seemed to be going well. Burr was saying a lot of things that I felt ought to be said but were not right for me to say. Is Burr correct about Jefferson? I'm so glad I don't have to decide. Plato probably spoke truly when he said that poets are irresponsible.

Then in the years that followed, "Burr" slowly became part of a larger pattern that had to be completed. From the beginning I had been aware of ulterior motives for turning my poetry loose in history. I had been writing a sequence of personal poems (*Word from the Hills*, my second book) that seemed to me covertly historical, and now "Burr" seemed covertly personal. Telling an expanded story was an opportunity for more of this. "Gould" came into existence partly because money has played a large unpleasant role in my life. It was helpful that my favorite robber baron had been born in the year that Burr died; but it was a dead end, and the occasion for a whole poem that had to be destroyed, to discover that my father was born in the year that Gould died. My pact, it seemed, was to portray people known only in books. Or perhaps in this I was like the spirits in Dante who have no knowledge of the present.

Still, I was sure that I had to tell about the future as well as the past. And how was that to be done? It is, of course, absurd to say that history repeats itself. But as I have said, I am devoted to absurdities. Just as there were times in the past which seem to resemble the present in one way or another (comparisons are always limited), so there may be times in the past which resemble what we sense in our own future. This gives the poet the concrete image he needs. I needed a crumbling world, and that led back to Cleopatra—a different Cleopatra who, I discovered, had been haunting me since a Classical Civilization course in college.

But why Archimedes? There was my obsession with mathematics, which had been trying to worm its way into my poetry for decades (and had turned many a poem bad in the process), but there was also a pattern of growing inwardness in my characters. The pure civilized contemplative—the life of the mind—had to have a place.

Then in the last poem, as in music, it seemed right to return to the beginning: to Burr's elegant cynicism reincarnated, fulfilled at last, in Julius Caesar, seen in the "female light" in which Burr delighted: the wise Cleopatra, who puts an end to—dots the "I" of—all that male nonsense.

But I must be quiet. I would like to brag a little about the way the blank verse changes from character to character—the unrhymed couplets of Archimedes, the breathless chatter of Cleopatra—but I have talked too much already. Reader, what you have found in these poems, if anything, is as surely in them as what I find. I am but a reader of them now myself. I have lived since. The person who wrote them is a stranger.

RICHARD MOORE

ONTARIO REVIEW PRESS POETRY SERIES

A Gallery of Spiders
John R. Reed

Introducing Tom Wayman:
Selected Poems 1973-1980

Friend & Lover
John Ditsky

Introducing Eavan Boland

Empires
Richard Moore